HAVING
MOUNTAIN
MOVING
FAITH

HAVING MOUNTAIN MOVING FAITH

Living a success filled life

Akeam A. Simmons

HAVING MOUNTAIN MOVING FAITH
LIVING A SUCCESS FILLED LIFE

iUniverse books may be ordered through booksellers or by contacting:

iUniverse
1663 Liberty Drive
Bloomington, IN 47403
www.iuniverse.com
844-349-9409

Because of the dynamic nature of the Internet, any web addresses or links contained in this book may have changed since publication and may no longer be valid. The views expressed in this work are solely those of the author and do not necessarily reflect the views of the publisher, and the publisher hereby disclaims any responsibility for them.

Any people depicted in stock imagery provided by Getty Images are models, and such images are being used for illustrative purposes only. Certain stock imagery © Getty Images.

ISBN: 978-1-6632-4529-8 (sc)
ISBN: 978-1-6632-4530-4 (e)

Print information available on the last page.

iUniverse rev. date: 09/02/2022

God has dealt to every man the measure of faith

Romans 12:3

Now faith is the substance of things hoped for,
The evidence of things not seen

Hebrews 11:1

Contents

Foreword

Often we don't know how much faith we have until faith is our only option. I experienced this personally.... believe God or surrender and die.

I had been suffering with a quarter sized sore on my great toe. It wouldn't heal after four months, so I went to the doctor (after much coercion from my wonderful wife, for, what I thought, some medicine to help it heal. I thought that I would be in and out of his office in no time; and back to my normal routine, but little did I know, I was in for a most challenging experience filled with hurt, doubt, tears, and fears... saturated with spouts of faith.

After a series of X rays, Cat scans, and ultra sounds, the doctors told me that I had an infection to the bone and they put me in the hospital.

One morning, several doctors and surgeons stood at the foot of my hospital bed and conveyed to me how serious my condition was and what they were about to do.

"That toe is gone, and we'll probably have to cut a little further up your leg because the infection is spreading up your leg, and we're trying to catch it before it gets in your blood stream-this is a very serious infection Mr. Simmons."

"What?" I said in shock, and I kept on saying to myself-but it's just a little sore. "Can't we just wait and see what it does?"

"No, time is not on your side. We are surgeons; we cut off and amputate toes, feet, and legs; that's what we do and why we are here at your bedside." He said with no hint of compassion or empathy. I guess they are so accustom to serving bad news until they no longer have time for emotions.

They left my room, and I thousand thoughts reeled through my head. I just came to the doctor to get some salve and some pills for a little sore on my toe. I couldn't believe it.

My wife was weeping and praying, as she paced the floor back and forth by my bed. She cried out to God!

"Akeam, you can't let them just cut off your leg!" She lamented as streaks of sorrow filled tears raced down her cheeks and splashed upon her chest.

"This can't be happening. In a minute, I am going to wake up from this horrible dream." I said to myself, but it wasn't a dream; the sharp pains shooting up my leg and the IV of antibodies medicine flowing into my vein, and my weeping wife, made me accept that it wasn't a dream; this was real.

Sleep fled from me even after several doses of HYDROCODONE. I soon realized that it was quite easy to talk of having faith, but it is quite another thing when the crises sit in your lap, and is threatening to change your entire life, or even take your life.

Early the next morning, nine doctors stood around my bed-two surgeons, an infectious disease doctor, a wound specialist, a podiatrist, the chief doctor on staff, and three wide eyed curious student doctors that tried their very best to be incognito.

"Mr. Simmons, your situation is quite serious. The infection is to the bone and spreading up your leg. Our biggest concern now is to stop the infection from getting into your blood stream and becoming septic; that could cause you your life." The chief doctor said as he pressed a couple of his fingers down into my leg to see how much edema was there-his finger prints went deep into my leg and stayed there. He took out his pen and put a mark on my leg just below the knee, and then peered easily over at the surgeons while they, almost motionless, nodded their heads. I didn't realize it at the time, but they were agreeing that the surgeons should amputate from there.

I had never been that scared before in my life. Though Kim, my wife, wanted to stay over with me every night, I demanded that she went home for the night. I didn't want her to see me weep and become broken.

I prayed and prayed all night, but it seemed like heaven was silent and God was not taking any calls-at least not from me, I thought; like when Mary and Martha sent a letter to Jesus about Lazarus being sick, but He didn't answer nor go to see about him. The most difficult time is when an astute Believer is hollering out to God and it seems like God doesn't hear him, or He is outright ignoring him-but, in desperation, I kept ranging up heaven… it was my only option!

The next night, about 2 am, the nurse came in my room to take my vital signs. She simply freaked out when she read my blood pressure numbers.

"What? What's wrong?" I asked, more than a little concerned.

"Your, your blood pressure is 265 over 150." She said nervously, trying her best to now contain her emotions.

"So, what does that mean?" I nervously asked, more than a little concerned.

"You could have a stroke at any minute." She said while sticking the needle deep into my arm.

"What? Really?" I managed to say in a haze of confusion.

She gave me a shot and soon left my room.

It was then that I realized that I was under a spiritual attack. The devil was coming at me every way that he could. I realized that you have to be careful who you talk to about what you're going through-most folks don't know what to say in grave situations. Ninety-nine percent of the people that I spoke to always made me feel worst, though they thought that they were comforting me-even my clergy friends; they would say things like: Their mama, or daddy, or grandmother or somebody in their family had had their toe, foot, or leg cut off too; others would out right ask me if my foot was black, cause if it is black Reverend you've got gangrene, and one of the nurses just out right told me that I ought to gone and let the doctors cut my foot off and gone and get it over with so that I can heal and go on with life.

One of my friends, I simply hung up the phone on him with all of his negative energy; so I stopped answering the phone to save myself from all the good intentioned nay Sayers.

Friday morning the nurse came into my room and said that I could not eat anything after 12 am because I was going into surgery the next morning.

I started praying all that day because I kept asking myself when had I agreed to have surgery.

That night, in the darken solitude of my hospital room, I realized that I was going through a spiritual warfare. I lay there wounded physically, psychologically, and emotionally.

I could hear the devil speaking in the channels of my mind-tormenting me.

"Just look at you preacher: you have served God most of your life and look at the reward you get. You are lying here at the point of death and He won't even answer your prayer. You wasted your whole life for what-this?"

"The Lord rebukes you Satan!" I shouted aloud in the darkness, and then looked at my pain filled throbbing foot and pointed at it and shouted in anger, "You stop it! You stop it right now in the name of Jesus!" My foot soon stopped shooting pain up my leg.

The next morning, I was awakened by the surgeon. Again, he looked at my foot and then said, "I just don't see what the other doctors are seeing." He examined my foot again thoroughly. "We're not going to do surgery right now; we'll just watch it for a few more days and see if it responds to the antibody medicine. Besides, I couldn't if I wanted to because the entire operating room has been shut down."

I smiled and said excitedly, "Look at God!"

He just politely smiled at me.

"So, can I get something to eat now?"

I felt like God had shut the entire operating room down just so that they wouldn't make a mistake and operate on me-Look at God!

After many IV bags of antibodies pumped into my body, Monday morning they dismissed me with the instructions that I had a long ways to go, and they seriously doubted that I would be healed. They told me that I was putting off the inevitable.

I am still asking God for a complete healing, and I believe that He's going to heal me completely-either way, He is still my God, and nothing will lessen my faith in Him. I realize that there is always purpose in my suffering.

All of this over a wound that was no bigger than a quarter.

My journey has not fully ended as of yet, but I chose to try, as I go through, to help other Believers endure and walk through their trials with confidence - by acquiring MOUNTAIN MOVING FAITH!

In the darkness, in the lonely solitude of my room, it dawned on me that- The devil was trying to kill my faith, which was my only hope right now.

Forward

When I collectively consider all of man, it is conclusively apparent that "man" suffers from a lack of faith. He fails to realize that he is an entity of faith. Without faith, his quality of living decreases, or even, he ceases to exist altogether. My hospital stay made this crystal clear to me.

We were designed by our creator to live a high quality, productive, and a purpose filled life. You are not supposed to live a defeated and fearful life. You were created to succeed and have good (much) success. God told Cain, "If you don't do well, sin lies at your door." Sin is anything that is contrary to the purpose for which God created you for. In other words, it is in your nature to do well; to make it even plainer-you are supposed to succeed and have much success.

You see, you were made in His Image and after His likeness-you are just like God; and God, by virtue of who He is, is a manifesto of faith. If you want to know how you are to operate in life, just look at God. In the bible, Numbers 23: 19 says, God is not a man, that he should lie, neither the son of man, that he should repent: has he said, and shall he not do it: or has he spoken, and shall he not make it good? What that is saying is that God cannot lie, for He is the essence of faith. God is so full of faith until whatsoever He utters from His mouth automatically comes to be, even if it had not been before He spoke.

You cannot lie if whatever you say comes to be.

Observe, Genesis 1: 26-27:

> 26. And God said, Let us make man in our image, after
> our likeness: and let them have dominion over the fish

of the sea, and over the fowl of the air, and over the cattle, and over all the earth, and over every creeping thing that creeps upon the earth.

27. So God created man in his own image, in the image of God created he him; male and female created he them.

You were created to be just like your creator-whatever he says comes to pass. Whatever you believe with passion-truly believe, has to happen because you are just like the one that created you.

The problem is we have been trained throughout our lives, how not to believe, how not to live our faith in a faithful way. You've been taught to fear and live a defeatist life. And, if you were taught to fear and accept defeat so easily, then, you often time will teach your children the same. We must change that! We are faithless because our parents taught us to be faithless, just as their parents taught them to be faithless, and unless we change, we shall teach our children to be faithless-to only believe what they can see, touch, and fear. So thus, our lives have been full of fear because that's what we were taught. Rarely did we see faith at work, so we failed to see how faith worked; fear and desperation is the norm.

By God's design, you were created to live in faith; to believe, with passion, that whatsoever you expect will happen; that's your purpose, live a life of success filled with victory after victory.

God expects you to emulate Him-to show others how to live a fulfilling life filled with purpose.

It is the design of this book to assist you in living your faith so that you can live in your purpose and live a full life filled with success. It is already in you. It is just that you have been taught a life filled with doubt and fear, and so you truly have no idea "who" you are, and when you do not know who you are, you will adapt to someone else and they will tell you wrongfully who you are. You are a reflection of God upon the earth that men can see. They see God through you because they see God in you-working His power through you.

2 Corinthians 5: 7

7. For we walk by faith, not by sight.

When it says Walk, it means to live-to live beyond what you see, or what people are saying, or how things have always been. You change things first by changing you-how you think and see things, and when you do that, you will change your experience.

Just going to church every week will not, by itself, afford you to walk in victory; remember many people go to church every Sunday, or frequently, but still live lives of quiet defeat-even after shouting and speaking in tongues all day on Sunday.

Learn how to live your faith, and watch your whole world change!

*****Many of the main points, I have written numerous times in different parts of this book to stress their importance, and their power to you******

REMEMBER- GOD WILL NOT DO FOR YOU THAT
FOR WHICH YOU CAN DO FOR YOURSELF

YOU MUST CHOOSE TO AWAKEN YOUR FAITH,
AND IN ORDER TO DO THAT, YOU MUST
BECOME DISSATISFIED WITH WHERE YOU
ARE, OR ELSE YOU WILL NEVER CHOOSE TO
BELIEVE GOD OVER YOUR CIRCUMSTANES

Chapter One

TAKE A GOOD LOOK IN THE MIRROR

You've been living for others, trying to be like others, or just living up to the status quo (the norm in your environment) until you really don't rightly know who you are, and remember, when you fail to know who you are, somebody else will tell you who you are and what to believe; they will choose your destiny for you. And, you won't know what you are missing until you know what is yours, and what you have access to.

After the doctors had come in my room and given me the devastating news, I pulled the sheets up to my neck and curled up as if trying to hide from what I had to go through. Then, I heard a voice pierce the solemn silence.

"You can forget that big toe buddy because it's gone; the only question is how for up your leg are they gone cut off." My hospital roommate, an old Caucasian man with a long white beard, bellowed out. "But you'll be alright; you can get over it. I had mine cut off; you can come and look at it when you get time. It ain't that big of a deal."

I didn't respond. I just lay there filled with anger that he had the nerve to even address my situation-though he thought that he was helping me.

"Are you there?" He said, shuffling in his sheets.

:"Yea, I growled back," hoping that he would just shut up and keep his opinion to himself. I didn't want to talk to anybody-give me time to lick my ever emerging wounds.

"Well, when you get ready, come look at my leg."

I simply didn't reply; I knew that if I did say what I wanted to say; it would probably hurt his feelings.

"I heard the doctors say what medicine you're taking." He said, refusing to shut up. "Man, all that medicine is doing is killing you. You hear me? Stop taking all of it."

I still didn't answer him. Of all the men in the hospital that I could share a room with, they gave me a roommate from hell!

I still didn't answer him; and though he looked like Santa clause with his long white beard, he was no Santa Clause for me, because he only gave me morbid news.

I realized that you've got to access your own situation-look at you, and decide how you're going to fight this battle because if you don't, others will choose for you-and they usually won't choose what is best for you.

Until you look at you, I mean really take a good in-depth look at yourself, it will be impossible to cease the life that you live-or lack of life that you miss. When you don't realize who and what you are, you automatically devalue yourself and try to find self-fulfillment and self-worth in "things" and other people; which is why you find some people driving a Mercedes Benz with nowhere to park it, or carrying a Gucci purse with no money in it and no money in the bank, and why we buy expensive snickers, suits, shoes, and jewelry that we cannot afford. Society has trained you that it doesn't matter if you are broke and outdoors with no place to live, just as long as you look rich.

Subsequently, your life becomes a life filled with sickness, struggle, unhappiness, and misery. All you come to know is worry, depression, anxiety, sickness, disease, dependency, obsession, compulsive, and paranoia.

You will never change if you don't seek change, and to seek change, there has to be an awareness of lack and need. It is like when I was growing up as a kid, I didn't know that we were poor because everybody around me were poor; it was the norm in my neighborhood, so it was naturally accepted by all.

You see, when you see you, the real you, and come to understand who you were supposed to be, you acquire a yearning to change and walk in the purpose that your creator designed for you.

Well, who are you? To know yourself and your purpose, you have got to look at God's template for your life.

Observe what God said about you when He put the first man in creation: Genesis 1: 26-28:

> 26. And God said, let us make man in our image, after our likeness: and let them have dominion over the fish of the sea, and over the fowls of the air, and over cattle, and over all the earth, and over every creeping that creeps upon the earth.

> 27. So God created man in his own image, in the image of God created he him; male and female created he them.

> 28. And God blessed them, and God said unto them, be fruitful, and multiply, and replenish the earth, and subdue it: and have dominion over the fish of the sea, and over the fowl of the air, and over every living thing that moves upon the earth.

Now pay particular attention to four words in the text-there it describes who you are and what your character is to be:

1. Dominion
2. Subdue
3. Replenish
4. Blessed

Let us delve even further into these words to better understand what God was saying to us.

1. **Dominion** means sovereignty or control; the power to rule, or be in charge of something; to have supernatural power over everything. Thus, God gave you supernatural power and authority over everything.

2. **Subdue** means to conquer and bring into subjection-to vanquish. This means to put everything under you. Subdue all your situations, problems (don't allow a problem to be a problem, or remain a problem-subdue it). All things are subject to you and are under your control. Subdue means to gain control over something or someone. When you subdue something, you conquer, defeat, overcome, and reduce it; whether it is a person, or situation, or condition, or even a relationship that has gone afoul.

3. **Replenish** means to fill up again-to resupply and restore. You must be willing to bring back something that is dead or dying. You replenish by leading the way to higher plains. Replenish also means to assure a continuum of another just like you.

4. Blessed. You must always remember above everything else, that you are blessed. Having things and stuff in the world does not make you blessed; you might have those things because you are blessed. Note, the simplest meaning of the word blessed: to have

divine favor upon you-meaning that God looks favorably upon you. It also means that you are divinely touched by the most high, the most supreme God of the entire universe.

So hence, when you look in the mirror, you should truly see a reflection of God enveloped by flesh. You are a dominating, subduing, replenishing, blessed child of God that lives, moves, breathes buy faith every day.

It is highly important that you, as a child of God, must grasp this, for people will see in you no more than what you see in yourself; and, oftentimes they will not see, or refuse to see what you see. You must establish "who" you are, or who you want to become.

My hospital stay was four days of hell, but I chose it to be a growing, learning time for me-to "experience" my faith. It became no longer about my leg, but will I trust God, and have faith in His plan that He created just for me. Sometimes we fail to recognize that there is always purpose in your pain. God is very intentional. The storm didn't come to blow you away, but it did come to move you to a different place in God.

Your words to yourself confirm and affirm who you are. And, you must believe (in faith), you are who you say you are, and you are becoming deeper into that person you are-or hope to be.

Oftentimes, looking into your mirror, you must peer beyond what is, and see what you hope to become, discounting what outsiders feel about you, for they are not in your mirror unless you give them access.

Muhammad Ali said that every day he looks in the mirror and tells himself that he is the greatest fighter of all times; even after he had temporarily lost his world champion title to Joe Frazier. Although there was a new champion, Muhammad Ali still declared that he was the greatest, and he soon regained his title. He didn't allow others outside of himself to determine who he was.

And, you cannot allow others to dictate who you are because they will see a faltering failing you; oftentimes, because that is what they wish upon you.

Again, like Muhammad Ali, he said that he noticed this woman at every one of his fights. She would be on the front row. He thought to himself that she was a great fan of his because she was at all of his fights sitting on the front row. After one of his fights, he finally met the woman and told her how much he appreciated her being such a faithful fan and coming to all of his fights. She looked him sternly in the eyes, and with a snooty attitude, she said, "I am not a fan of yours, I just want to be there when you get knocked out." Ali was stunned. **Just because people seem to be on your team, does not mean that they are on your side.**

So, you can't depend on others to see the greatness in you; you must see it in yourself even before it manifests itself-through the eyes of your mountain moving faith that Jesus spoke of. Remember, faith is the substance of things hoped for, and the evidence of things not seen-substance is the matter in which something exist, and evidence is the proof that it exist. In other words your faith brings things to life even when in the natural they have not manifested yet. So, the Apostle Paul was saying that everything that you need is in your faith, even when in the natural you can't see it, but the proof is in your faith.

Note, when you observe yourself in a physical mirror, there is also a lot of things showing up in the mirror in the background. You must not allow those things to distract you from what you want to see-focus on "you" and what you want to become. There is so much stuff in your background and around you that if you continue to pay attention to them, they will nullify and kill your faith-what you are believing to change and come forth in your life.

The first step of faith, is first seeing and recognizing you; who you are right now, and then purposely changing; in your heart, see what you desire to see and even more manifestations to come.

If you don't determine "who" you are, and "whose" you are then someone else will determine who you are and decide your fate for you.

It is important that you determine within yourself who you see in the mirror, and if you see yourself and don't like what you see, then change it. Only you can change you. They often times say that opposites attract, but that is only partially true. Truth be told, things that are most alike are attracted to each other. So it is with you; what you are is what you attract to you. If you are bitter, then you will attract bitter people; if you are hateful, you will attract hate; if you are friendly, you will attract friends, if you are broken, you will attract broken people.

When you look in your mirror, you must always see a work in progress. You are "becoming". How you see yourself in your own mirror is often how others will see you. If you see an unworthy person, then that's what others will see in you; if you see a mighty person that is an overcomer that is confident in themselves and loving of others.

The bible says: Joel 3: 10:

> Beat your plowshares into swords, and your pruning
> hooks into spears: let the weak say, I am strong.

He was talking to farmers becoming warriors; See yourself as a warrior and a conqueror; and you shall soon become one.

Only you can change what you see in your mirror.

Look at yourself every day in the mirror, and determine what and who you want to see; discount what you see in the back ground, and keep telling yourself what you want to see and be in your life. You were created with purpose! Yes, you have faltered; yes, you have failed continuously, you cannot change what happened to you yesterday, but you can affect your tomorrows. Now, right now, is the most opportune time to change what you see in your mirror, thereby creating a new world for you...........Your world will only reflect who and what you see in the mirror.

Chapter Two

GOD'S KIND OF FAITH

You must believe in something supernatural
That's greater than yourself
That's outside of yourself…GOD

FAITH WITHOUT WORKS IS DEAD
FAITH MUST BE ACCOMPANIED BY WORK

WHATEVER YOU BELIEVE WITH PASSION
YOU WILL SOON SEE COME TO FRUITION
YOU EXPERIENCE WHATEVER YOU BELIEVE

If you only believe in yourself and only what you can do, or have done, you will go no further than where you are, and no further than where you have already been.

In order to get to the mountain, you must be willing to go through the valley.

The bigger the mountain, the deeper the valley- Faith is built in the valleys of life and exercised on the conquered mountains of success.

I lay on my hospital bed deflated and defeated. For over forty years I had been preaching to others about the importance of faith; but, here I was struggling to keep my faith.

The doctor's faith was the only way to save my life was to amputate my toe, foot, leg or something-they were sure of it, and was trying their very best to convince me. They acted as though they were getting commission for every amputation they did.

I was screaming to God, but God was silent. My faith was slowly seeping away.

That evening, I sent my wife home because I didn't want her to see me so weak, and I didn't want her to see my sorrow besiege me while I wept. Somehow and some way, I had to rejuvenate my faith.

T HE ONLY WAY TO BELIEVE IN something that is greater than yourself and is outside of yourself is through what is referred to as **FAITH**. It is so powerful until it supersedes even religion, though it is the very essential fiber of it. Whatever you acquire or do not acquire is the end result of your faith.

Faith is so extremely important in our lives until The Apostle Paul discusses it extensively in his letter to the Hebrews.

Note Hebrews 11: 1-6:

> 1. Now faith is the substance of things hoped for, the evidence of things not seen.

> 2. For by it the elders obtained a good report.

> 3. Through faith we understand that the worlds were framed byy the word of God, so that things which are seen were not made of things which do appear,

> 4. By faith Abel offered unto God a more excellent sacrifice than Cain, by which he obtained witness that he was righteous, God testifying of his gifts: and by it he being dead yet speaks.

> 5. By faith Enoch e=was translated that he should not see death; and was not found, because God had translated him: for before his translation he had this testimony, that he pleased God.

> 6. But without faith it is impossible to please him: for he that comes to God must believe that he is, and that he is a rewarder of them that diligently seek him.

Note, he instructs us that everything that we need to accomplish by faith is encapsulated in our faith. Paul says that faith is the substance and evidence of what you are believing God for. **SUBSTANCE** is the real physical matter of something. Your faith materializes it and makes it tangible and believable. The **EVIDENCE** is proof that it exist.

All that you need to turn your life around and conquer those things that plague you, those things that's been hindering you, and reach those things that simply seems to have been out of your reach, is faith.

But, faith, in order for it to work, it has to be accompanied by works. If you say that you believe it, then you must walk in what you believe. Expect it to come to pass. Example, if you are believing God for food, you must get up and set the table; if you are believing for a better job, you must start searching for the job, and God will bring it to fruition; if you are looking for a spouse, carry yourself in such a way that shows that you are good marriage material that is looking for a good partner.

Observe what the Apostle James says of the matter on faith and works: James 2: 14-20:

> 14. What does it profit, my brother, though a man say he has faith, and have not works? Can faith save him?

> 15. If a brother or sister be naked and destitute of daily food,

> 16. And one of you say to him depart and go in peace, be you warmed and filled, not withstanding, you give them not those things which are needful to the body; what does it profit.

> 17. Even so, faith if it has not works, is dead being alone.

18. Yea, a man may say, You have faith, and I have works; show me your faith without your works, and I will show you my faith by my works.

19. You believe that there is one God; you do well: the devils also believe, and tremble.

20. But will you know, O vain man, that faith without works is dead?

The Apostle James is stressing the importance of faith and work moving in unison to accomplish the believer's desires.

Faith is not something that just automatically comes because you know God; no, you have got to purposely "live" your faith; endeavor each and every day to walk by faith.

You can have a relationship with God and still live a quiet life of defeat; yes, you can be saved, sanctified, Holy Spirit filled, and fire baptized, but if you do not choose to live your faith with works, you will live beneath who God purpose you to be. Without faith and works, you will live a quiet life of defeat, even though you are saved.

The Apostle Paul says that "Now faith is the substance". Faith is always in the "now"; and it is always filled with substance to bring about what you believe.

So, each day, purpose to live your faith, and starve your doubts so that you can accomplish all that God purposed for you.

Chapter Three

RECOGNIZE THE MOUNTAINS IN YOUR LIFE

My mountain was not all those nay saying doctors around my hospital bed that were anxious to cut off something; no, my mountain was maintaining a Godly, Holy Spirit filled state of mind through it all. God, in your life cannot be reduced to Him saving you, or His willingness and ability to save you. No, He must still be your God even if He chooses not to save you. The three Hebrew boys in the fiery furnace awesome statement was, "We know that God has the power to save us, but if He chooses not to, we still are not going to bow down to any other god."

Although He has the power to change my situation, but chooses not to, my faith is still in Him; for I know that He chooses what's best for me.

Jesus elaborated on the matter further; note what He says in the Gospel of Matthew 5: 29-30:

> 29. And if your right eye offend you, pluck it out, and cast it from you; for it is profitable for you that one of your members should perish, and not that your whole body should be cast into hell.

> 30. And if your right hand offend you, cut t off, and cast it from you; for it is profitable for you that one of your members should perish, and not that your whole body should be cast into hell.

So thus, my mountain was not whether or not I lose a toe, or foot, or leg, the mountain that embraced me was how to hold on to my faith through it all, in- spite of the outcome.

MOUNTAIN IS A SYNONYM FOR ANYTHING that gets in your way and causes you to deviate from God's plan for you. A mountain in your life is that which causes you to live outside of your destiny and your purpose or anything that hinders you from a healthy wealthy life (your best life) full of joy, peace, love, and fulfillment- whether it is sickness, finance, relationships, trouble, confusion, or even religion; whatever stops you from living a full wholesome happy and joy filled life is a mountain that you must deal with properly. You see, you are already dealing with it; just not the right way; so it is conquering you instead of you conquering it.

Remember what God said to Cain in Genesis 4: 7: If you don't do well, sin lies at your door.

In other words, we are supposed to do well "prosper". If we are not doing well, it is because of sin (mountains). Some mountains we choose, and other mountains we inherit- either way we must move them out of our way.

The problem is many folks learn to ignore their mountains, or learn to accept it and live with it, but you will never live successfully in your purpose and destiny or have fulfilled happiness until you deal with the mountains in your life. Ignoring them won't make them go away.

Note what Jesus tells us about dealing with the mountains in our lives:

Matthew 21: 21-22:

> 21. Jesus answered and said unto them, Verily I say unto you, if you have faith, and doubt not, you shall not only do this which is done to the fig tree, but also if you shall say unto this mountain, Be you removed, and be you cast into the sea: it shall be done.

22. And all things, whatsoever you shall ask in prayer, believing, you shall receive.

Mark 11: 22-24:

22. And Jesus answering said unto them, Have faith in God.

23. For verily I say unto you that whosoever shall say unto this mountain, Be you removed and be you cast into cast into the sea; and shall not doubt in his heart, but shall believe that those things which he says shall come to pass.

24. Therefore I say unto you what things so ever you desire, when you pray, believe that you receive them, and you shall have them.

Remember, a mountain is anything that is in your way; anything that steals your peace, joy, love, happiness, and finance is a mountain to you.

Jesus tells us to get out of denial; it's a mountain. Don't deny it; call it what it is-a mountain that is in your way. It is not "your" mountain, so get rid of it. You'll never see what God has for you if you don't move that mountain; it obstructs your view.

Stop making excuses for that mountain that you are facing daily. If you are in a loveless relationship, stop settling for less, and stop making excuses for "why" they don't love you; as long as you make excuses for that mountain, it will never move, and if you won't move it, it will always be in the way of the true love that you really deserve; for as long as that mountain is there, it will always separate you from the one that will truly love you for you, and treat you with the love and respect that you so rightly deserve.

Yes, sometimes your past can even be a mountain in your present life. Sure, you've made many mistakes in your life, and perhaps done some awful things and it has become the mountain that you face today; it is getting in your way "today". No matter how hard you try, you will never change what happened in your past, or who you were in your past; yesterday will always contain what happened yesterday, and you cannot change it, but do not allow it to become a mountain that stops you from a fulfilling life. Make new "today" and learn from yesterday; Let it be a trophy to you for what not to do and what not to allow in your life.

Don't blame your mother, your father, or anyone in your family for your difficulties or inadequacies, or else, you make them your mountain. You must tell yourself that they did the best that they could with what they had, or even, they made some horrible decisions that hurt you. But, do not allow what they did, or failed to do, become a mountain to you.

You have failed in the past, and will, no doubt, suffer some degree of failure in the future, but when you fall, determine to fall "forward". Let your failures push you forward; and it is really not a complete failure, for you learned not to do that again.

When you recognize the mountain, call it what it is and commence to tearing it down.

Some religions are mountains, for they too often stop you from experiencing freedom in God. Your religion is supposed to foster for you a better relationship with God, thereby having a better relationship with your fellow man. Notice what the Bible says about religion: James 1: 27:

Pure religion and undefiled before God and the Father is this, To visit the fatherless and widows in their affliction, and to keep himself unspotted from the world.

Hence, the Apostle James says that real religion is being clean with God, caring for the fatherless and widows, and to keep yourself from being affected adversely by the world.

Remember, move your mountains, and don't let nothing or anybody become a mountain to you. Do not settle for the mountain because it has always been there, and you have gotten accustom to it. Always remember that it is a hindrance designed to terminate your purpose and destiny!

YOU MUST CONQUER THE MOUNTAINS IN YOUR LIFE IF YOU WANT TO LIVE YOUR BEST LIFE!!!

Chapter Four

THE POWER OF YOUR WORDS

LIFE AND DEATH IS IN THE POWER OF YOUR TONGUE

Proverbs 18: 21

THE GREATEST POWER THAT YOU POSSESS IS THE WORDS THAT PROCEED OUT OF YOUR MOUTH

Note, King Solomon's words in Proverbs 18: 20-21:

> 20. A man's belly shall be satisfied with the fruit of his mouth; and with the increase of his lips shall he be filled.

> 21. Death and life are in the power of the tongue: and they that love it shall eat the fruit thereof.

IN OTHER WORDS, YOUR WORDS ARE filled with explosive power, even when you are not aware of it. They bind you, or set you free; they will bring things to you or keep things from you. You must taste your words very carefully before they exit your lips; when they leave your lips, they search the atmosphere to bring to you what you have spoken.

There is no such thing as casual conversation! And, you must be cautious of who is talking to you, for most conversations are planting seeds in your life. Your words are life changing and life altering. Observe what Jesus says of the matter: John 7: 37-38:

> 37. In the last day, that great day of the feast, Jesus stood and cried, saying, If any man thirst, let him come unto me, and drink.

> 38. He that believes on me, as the scripture has said, out of his belly shall flow rivers of living water.

Jesus was not talking of physical water; no, He was speaking of the words that come out of your mouth; they are supposed to be life giving words (living waters). This means two things: 1. your words are to bring you life 2. Somebody else is supposed to be drinking from the well that flows out of you.

Your words change your life and anybody that listens to you!

You see, child of God, words are seeds that grow in you and effect a change outside of you. Hence, you must be very careful what proceeds out of your mouth, and who it is that is pouring into you.

If all you say is that you can't, then, you never will. If you associate with toxic people that is always reminding you of what you can't do and what not to expect, then you will never accomplish more than what you have already done.

You are not limited by where you are, or where you come from, for what you constantly speak, produces results that can propel you forward and help you escape the stricken state that you might be in.

I am and you are the child of The King; and you are destined to live the life for which you desire-as the King's children. That is why when Jesus entered a city and addressed the people, he would always say that The Kingdom of heaven is at hand. He was not talking about God's throne some place away in the heavens; no, He was speaking of citizenship in the authority and power of God right here on earth. Your words are backed up by the power and might of the most High God.

King David was telling us the power that we possess in God when he penned the 24th numbers of Psalms; note verse 1: The earth is the Lord's, and the fullness thereof; the world, and they that dwell therein.

David was telling us that the world and everything and everybody belong to God; thus, as His children, everything that is on the earth or in the earth belongs to us-God's children.

Observe how he ends the 24th numbers of the Psalm: verse 7. Lift up your heads, oh you gates: and be you lift up, you everlasting doors: and the King of glory shall come in.

First, he says that we are gates! A gate is designed to allow some things in and keep other things out. And, he says lift up your head. We lift our heads up in expectation.

David says that if you lift your head up, the King of glory shall come in and answer your prayers.

Look up with expectation and what you are looking for shall come forth from the well inside of you.

Say it, believe it, see it, expect it, and it shall come to pass.

You must feed your faith, and starve your doubts. Align yourself with folks that will pour into you, and help you believe in-spite of what you see.

Look out in front of you, and mentally see what you are believing God for, and keep professing it, and it shall come to pass.

Child of God, you must see it (your hopes and desires) in your cognizant mind before it manifests itself before you.

If all you see is what you see before you, then, you will never acquire all of God's best. You will only have what you have always had.

It all begins and ends with the words that are in you, that proceeds out of your mouth.

Our words bring life to what we truly believe.

Your words will either tear down the negative mountains in your life, or build new ones.

If you are sick, speak wellness; if you are in poverty, or need more financial stability, then, speak wealth. If you see a fulfilling relationship, then speak a change in your present life; if single and desire marriage, speak into existence a wonderful caring attentive mate, then, look for them, and God will send them.

IF WHEN YOU LOOK, YOU ONLY SEE WHAT YOU SEE
THEN YOU WILL ONLY HAVE WHAT
YOU HAVE ALWAYS HAD

A word spoken continuously will change your entire life!

But, words by themselves are not enough; your words must be accompanied by works! The audio and video of your life must be in sink to each other. Thus, what you are doing must line up with what you are saying; else they cancel each other out.

I cannot count how many times that I have heard some young person say to me that they are going to be a doctor; a brain surgeon, an aerospace engineer, a lawyer, or any highly successful person, but their activities do not line up with what they are confessing; so they end up failing miserably, and settle for something for less than their dreams. The profession looks good and it sounds good to say that that is what you are aspiring to be, but one has to put in the work "to become".

Faith filled words require work!

Many times it requires great sacrifices. Yes, you have to go to class and make above average grades, and excel as best you can; then, you can become the brain surgeon, aerospace engineer or lawyer, but it begins and finishes with hard work-**say it and do it!**

Like the woman wanting a good husband; first, she has to be willing to be by herself; cause God will never send the good man as long as you are still connected to someone else. She cannot expect a king when she is not a queen because every king desires a queen; so she has to invest in herself and present herself as a queen, and thus, the king will find her.

You've heard the old saying that says opposites attract. I beg to differ; likeness attract. Things are attracted to those things that are most like themselves.

When you align your actions with what you are saying, the universe will send to you what you desire.

Words in Faith with works always work! Say it, see it believe it, and it shall find you.

The power of words is immeasurable.

Note what the Bible says in the book of Joel 3: 10:

Beat your plowshares into swords, and your pruning hooks into spears; let the weak say, I am strong.

Here is what God was telling them: even though you all are just a bunch of farmers and are weak and know nothing about war and fighting, change your words and declare and confess that you are strong. He is telling them of the power of their words being able to turn somebody that is weak and feeble into mighty warrior-just by their words!

God will not do for you that for which you can do for yourself!

Taste your words before they exit your mouth, and make sure that they are saturated with faith and accompanied by works, then, whatever mountain is in your way shall be moved!

Continue to "say" what you are believing God for and what you are expecting Him to do in your life. Do not entertain any words from anybody outside of what you are confessing. Get rid of the "buts" in your life.

Other people, sometimes, even those that are closes to you will bring in negative "buts" in your word of faith.

They'll say to you, "Yea, but", "But you got to be realistic", "But this has never happened before", "But you need to accept your situation", "But God didn't promise that".

The list goes on and on, and if truth be told, everyone can find a "but" to justify their lack of faith.

Truth be told, sometimes you just need to change your friends and associates; for some folks are satisfied where they are, and they have gotten use to the lack, or struggle, or sickness, or whatever their situation is. They become what they are going through. So, you cannot afford to keep long company with them. Remember, you will be no more than the people you constantly associate with.

Many doctor's children become doctors, and a lot of lawyer's children become lawyers because that is what they have associated with all of their lives. When you check the records, most educated parents produce educated children. So is it in our daily lives. If you connect yourself with great achievers, you will soon become a great achiever-that's what you have become accustom to.

If you choose the right people and cut off all of those negative ones, you will soon acquire and become what you are believing God for; they will help keep you on track even when they are not intentionally trying; and, other times, they will help you to see that you are bigger than your situation or environment, but it all starts in you and the power that you put in your words.

Your associates will help you come up and come out, or they will help you accept where you are, and make excuses with you.

This is greatly illustrated in the book of 2 Kings 6: 15-17:

> 15. And when the servant of the man of God was risen early, and gone forth, behold, and host compassed the city both with horses and chariots. And his servant said unto him, Alas, my master! How shall we do?
>
> 16. And he answered, Fear not: for they that be with us are more than they that be with them.
>
> 17. And Elisha prayed, and said, Lord, I pray thee, open his eyes, that he may see. And the Lord opened the eyes of the young man; and he saw: and, behold, the mountain was full of horses and chariots of fire round about Elisha.

This servant was overcome by what he saw with his natural eyes; he could see no way out. So, old man Elisha prayed for God to open his spiritual eyes and see that they had more angels on their side than they had enemies coming up against them.

You've got to **"open your eyes"** and see the opportunities that God has laid before you.

The servant could only see so much; he needed the old man, Elisha, to assist him in seeing what he needed to see. His fear and worry was for nothing.

You need associates to help you see that you can come out, and that it is not going to be this way always-just keep on believing and saying what you believe. There is much **power in your words!**

If you want your mountains to move out of your way, then your words and actions must align with each other.

And do not recite those "sound good" poisonous prayers that you hear some people praying-you've, no doubt, heard them. They say, "Lord don't move my mountain; just give me the strength to climb." No! Jesus said not to try to climb your mountains; tell the mountain to move and be cast into the sea, and if you believe, that mountain will do what you have instructed it to do-get out of your way.

Say it ......Say it.............Say it......Say it, until your words bear fruit. Remember, you will have what you say you have.

Chapter Five

KINGDOM MINDED EQUALS KINGDOM LIVING

By the second day in the hospital, the doctor sent me down for a CT scan- a diagnostic imaging procedure that uses a combination of X-rays and computer technology to produce images of the inside of my leg. They found that, along with the bone infection, I had two abscesses in my leg-one in my great toe and one in the center of my foot-no wonder my leg had swollen to three times its size.

It seemed that there came one bad news after another. Again, I realized that this was no ordinary natural situation. I was under an evil spiritual attack, and if I did what I had always done (let it work itself out), I would perish.

I had to change my focus, and become Kingdom minded-it was my only salvation. I could choose to just lie there and take things as they come, or choose my destiny for myself and become, as Jesus so eloquently put it, kingdom minded. It had nothing to do with me being healed, though it was not entirely left out, but all to do with my status in God-my divine citizenship. Kingdom is a country, state, or territory ruled by a king. When I gave my life to Jesus, I became a citizen of heaven, though I am still upon earth, with all the rights and previleges of the king.

When you walk in kingdom living, you walk under the power and authority of the king............I declare my situation is changed, and my Father God is ordering my steps to make me better. In kingdom living, that which was designed to kill you, will give you life, even abundant life; that's what I chose in the silent darkness of my hospital room.

J ESUS OFTEN TALKED ABOUT **KINGDOM LIVING**. Note what He says in the book of Mark 1: 14-15:

> 14. Now after that John was put in prison, Jesus came into Galilee, preaching the gospel of the kingdom of God,

> 15. And saying, The time is fulfilled, and the kingdom of God is at hand: repent you, and believe the gospel.

Most folks believe that Jesus was talking about heaven-God's thrown, but He was talking about a new way of thinking and believing; a new way of living.

Now notice what Jesus calls His new doctrine-The gospel of the kingdom of God. Observe closer; gospel literally means good news, and the kingdom of God means that which God rules and that which is under His authority. Thus, what Jesus was saying is that He had good news of how we can change our lives by operating under God's authority.

This teaching is different from all other teachings before it; which is why He tells them to repent first. You can't understand and accept this new doctrine unless you repent first. Unlike the belief of most people, particularly Christian believers, repent, in its simplest term, means to change, to turn around, or to start over.

In other words, in order for you to understand and receive this divine good news, you've got to change the way you have been trained to think and act.

Jesus was not talking about heaven, God's thrown; He was talking about heaven fulfilled on earth-walking and living in the authority of God on earth.

Observe Jesus conversation on the matter in Luke 17: 20-21:

> 20. And when he was demanded of the Pharisees, when the kingdom of God should come, he answered them and said, The kingdom of God comes not with observation:

> 21. Neither shall they say, Lo here! Or, lo there! For, behold, the kingdom of God is within you.

Yes, yes, it's in you; planted deep in your heart, but no one taught you that, so that is the reason Jesus says that you got to repent-change; turn around and abandon your old way of thinking and believing.

All that you need to move the mountains in your life is already inside of you.

This principle did not just start with Jesus; it was also during Joshua's time. Note Joshua 1: 2-3:

> 2. Moses my servant is dead; now therefore arise, go over this Jordan, you, ad all this people, unto the land which I do give to them, even to the children of Israel.

> 3. Every place that the sole of your foot shall tread upon, that have I given unto you, as I said unto Moses.

You have got to believe beyond what you have been taught all of your life. Kingdom living is possessing all that God has for you right here, right now. You don't have to wait to get to heaven to experience God's kingdom.

Note God tell them that every piece of ground that they shall step on in the land of Canaan, he has already given it to them. That means that they already owns it, but there is a catch; they have got to set foot on it.

God puts "shall" and "given" together, but they denotes different time spans. "Shall" is future tense, and "given" is past tense. Hence, even though He has given it to them, it's not theirs until they set foot on it.

So are the principles of God in our lives (kingdom living). It works only if you apply it.

Remember, you can be saved, sanctified, spirit filled, fire baptized, and go to heaven when you die, but if you don't purposely apply kingdom living principles in your life, you will live a life of quiet defeat, and conquered by all the mountains coming up against you; which God didn't plan for you. That is what Jesus was talking about when He spoke of the Kingdom of heaven.

Kingdom living and kingdom minded means that you are moving the mountains in your life by God's authority and provision. Your faith and your will must line up to His declared word.

Everybody and everything is affected by God-your circumstances, condition, situation-God can alter everything as He pleases.

Why? Well, look at Psalms 24: 1:

> 1. The earth is the Lord's, and the fullness thereof; the world, and they that dwell therein.

When you are kingdom minded, you expect and believe that God will operate on your behalf and move the mountains out of your way.

Mountains are a distraction from your will to believe in and worship God almighty. They get in the way of you achieving and receiving God's best for you.

The kingdom of heaven is at hand; now make your mountains be casted into the sea, and go live the life intended for all of God's children.

Repent, change your thought life; force yourself to see things differently, and accept God's word into your life, then watch Him change your life and move all of those crippling mountains out of your way.

It has been said that seeing is believing, but in kingdom living, it is believing is seeing. You believe it, accept it, and thank God for it even before it manifest in your life.

You are a citizen of the kingdom of heaven, and as a citizen, you have rights- kingdom rights. Now, rise up and declare your rights and walk in them expectantly.

Chapter Six

YOU MUST HAVE AN ACTIVE PRAYER LIFE

ALONE, IN MY HOSPITAL ROOM, GOD AND I
HAD LONG SERIOUS CONVERSATIONS THAT I
NEVER TOOK TIME FOR BEFORE-NOW, HE HAD
MY COMPLETE UNDEVIDED ATTENTION
AND I LISTENED, TRULY LISTENED
TO WHAT HE SAID

1kings 19: 12 says God speaks in a small still voice,
so when conversing (praying) with Him, you must
listen intently-listen more that you speak

B EFORE WE JOURNEY ANY FURTHER IN this discourse on prayer, let us first discover just what prayer is. Prayer, in its basic definition, is an individual, or group of people, having a conversation with God.

Although many people that pray, usually talk to God in a monologue (they do all the talking and never listen to what God has to say to them). Prayer, that gets results, is a dialogue between the individual and God-you say something to God, and then listen to what God has to say to you.

Prayer builds intimacy between you and God, which affords you the opportunity to really see God in His fullness-His glory, his power, and his majesty.

Prayer is so very important until Jesus instructed, verbatim, His disciples how to pray; note Matthew 6: 9-13:

> 9. After this manner therefore pray you: Our Father which are in heaven, Hallowed be your name.

> 10. Your kingdom come. Your will be done in earth, as it is in heaven.

> 11. Give us this day our daily bread.

> 12. And forgive us our debts, as we forgive our debtors

> 13. And lead us not into temptation, but deliver us from evil: For yours is the kingdom, and the power, and the glory, forever. Amen.

Many people pray this prayer, but this was not for Christians today. Jesus taught this prayer to His disciples as a transitional prayer-to keep them while He was completing His work of redeeming man of his sins. When we say that prayer, it becomes a recital with no power. That prayer was to keep them until He had bridged the gap again between God the Father and earthly man.

Your prayer life has to be personal with God-not a recital, but a sincere conversation where you expose your deepest self to God-your wounds, your pain, your hurts, your disappointments, your tears, your sorrows, and desires all mingled with your gratitude.

Prayer is personal. Your prayer is different from others because your needs and wants are different. Most of the time, you are in a different place and going through different things than your neighbors. Your prayer has to be personal and filled with sensation. Observe what Jesus says of your intimate prayer with the Father: Matthew 7: 7-8:

> 7. Ask, and it shall be given you; seek, and you shall find; knock, and it shall be opened unto you:

> 8. For every one that aske receives; and he that seeks finds; and to him that knocks, it shall be opened.

Prayer is asking, seeking, and knocking; asking God for something and seeking His answer while you knock on doors in faith, believing that God is going to answer your prayer.

In other words, my prayer, my conversation with God, covers all of me-my needs, my aspirations, and even my wants and desires are all in my intimate conversation with God.

My relationship and prayer to God even affects the world around me. Notice what God says to us of how our prayers are filled with power. 2 Chronicles 7: 14-15:

> 14. If my people, which are called my name, shall humble themselves, and pray, and seek my face, and turn from their wicked ways; then will I hear from heaven, and will forgive their sin, and will heal their land.

> 15. Now mine eyes shall be open, and mine ears attend unto the prayer that is made in this place.

This is God talking. He didn't say that if the world would come together, or if the Democrats and the Republicans would agree, but only His people-people that pray to Him and worship Him. Hence, God says that our prayer life, our intimate conversation with Him can change the world. The world is messed up because God's children have ceased to pray for it-Prayer changes things, circumstances, conditions, and even people.

Don't try to understand the situation, or the people; just lift up your hearts to God in prayer, and He will change whatever needs changing.

Jesus also said that there is power when fellow believers come together and pray (prayer partner). Matthew 18: 18-20:

> 18. Verily I say unto you, whatsoever you shall bind on earth shall be bound in heaven; and whatsoever you shall loose on earth shall be loosed in heaven.

19. Again I say unto you, that if two of you shall agree on earth as touching anything that they shall ask, it shall be done for them of my Father which is in heaven.

Understand this: Jesus says that "whatever" you say on earth, heaven hears you and agrees with you. If you bind and loose it on earth, God's kingdom and His power agree with you and bind and loose it in heaven.

So, get you a prayer partner-somebody that is praying with you and believing with you; and, you are praying with them and believing with them.

One of our biggest mistakes is that we think that God is going to do what we need Him to do anyway. But, that is not true. Look at what is said in the book of James 4: 2-3:

2. You lust, and have not: you kill, and desire to have, and cannot obtain: you fight and war, yet you have not, because you ask not.

3. You ask, and receive not, because you ask amiss, that you may consume it upon your lusts.

Here is what James is saying; sometimes we don't have what we need and want because we fail to pray for them, or when we do pray, our prayers are not specific.

Sometimes, when we pray, we say those nonspecific prayers; like, "God, I ask that you bless me real good". What is that-real good? That's a nonspecific prayer. You must be specific! If you are praying for a house, go find the house that you would like to have, and then ask God for it. Like, "Dear Lord bless me with the house on (the color and address of the house). See, that is asking and being specific.

Be very careful how you pray to God. Haven't you heard people pray, "God don't move my mountain, just give me the strength to climb." That is crazy praying. No, you want the mountain out of your way!

Prayer, intimate conversation with God, opens doors for us, and close some doors that have let some things in our lives that wasn't good for us.

Understand this: Jesus says that "whatever" you say on earth, heaven hears you and agrees with you. If you bind and loose it on earth, God's kingdom and His power agrees with you and bind and loose it in heaven- God gives it the power to be and become.

God brings to existence whatever you say with passion.

You must remember erase that proverbial saying that you have been told over and over again-opposites attract each other. No! "likeness" attract each other. In other words, you draw to you whatever you are and whatever you release into the atmosphere. If you claim blessings, blessings are drawn to you; if you claim poverty, poverty will find you; if you claim sickness, wealth, health, or whatever, the atmosphere will send it to you.

If you don't like where you are, or what you are getting, then change what you are releasing in your life and around you; whatever you release, comes back to you.

And too, get you a prayer partner-somebody that is praying with you and believing with you; and, you are praying with them and believing with them.

One of our biggest mistakes is that we think that God is going to do what we need Him to do anyway. But, that is not true. Look at what is said in the book of James 4: 2-3:

1. You lust, and have not: you kill, and desire to have, and cannot obtain: you fight and war, yet you have not, because you ask not.

2. You ask, and receive not, because you ask amiss, that you may consume it upon your lusts.

Here is what James is saying; sometimes we don't have what we need and want because we fail to pray for them, or when we do pray, our prayers are not specific.

Sometimes, when we pray, we say those nonspecific prayers; like, "God, I ask that you bless me real good". What is that-real good? That's a nonspecific prayer. You must be specific! If you are praying for a house, go find the house that you would like to have, and then ask God for it. Like, "Dear Lord bless me with the house on (the color and address of the house). See, that is asking and being specific.

Be very careful how you pray to God. Haven't you heard people pray, "God don't move my mountain, just give me the strength to climb." That is crazy praying. No, you want the mountain out of your way!

Prayer, intimate conversation with God, opens doors for us, and closes some doors that have let some things in our lives that weren't good for us.

God hears, and God cares, so He honors what you say
to Him, and gives you what is best for you according
to His will.

Understand this: Jesus says that "whatever" you say on earth, heaven
hears you and agrees with you. If you bind and loose it on earth, God's
kingdom and His power agree with you and bind and loose it in heaven.

So, get you a prayer partner-somebody that is praying with you and
believing with you; and, you are praying with them and believing with
them.

Again, one of our biggest mistakes is that we think that God is going
to do what we need Him to do anyway. But, that is not true. Look at
what is said in the book of James 4: 2-3:

> 1. You lust, and have not: you kill, and desire to have,
> and cannot obtain: you fight and war, yet you have not,
> because you ask not.

> 2. You ask, and receive not, because you ask amiss, that
> you may consume it upon your lusts.

Here is what James is saying; sometimes we don't have what we need
and want because we fail to pray for them, or when we do pray, our
prayers are not specific.

Sometimes, when we pray, we say those nonspecific prayers; like, "God,
I ask that you bless me real good". What is that-real good? That's a
nonspecific prayer. You must be specific! If you are praying for a house,
go find the house that you would like to have, and then ask God for it.
Like, "Dear Lord bless me with the house on (the color and address of
the house). See, that is asking and being specific.

Be very careful how you pray to God. Haven't you heard people pray, "God don't move my mountain, just give me the strength to climb." That is crazy praying. No, you want the mountain out of your way! You must want the stumbling blocks out of your way! Jesus said to tell the mountain to move; why are you praying for strength to climb it?

Prayer, intimate conversation with God, opens doors for us, and closes some doors that have let some things in our lives that weren't good for us.

The greatest travesty that befalls man is he fails to realize "who" he is, therefore, he does not know the power that he possess or what is readily at his disposal. There is power in his words because of who he is. Why? Because of whom he is. Look at the book of Psalms 82: 5-7:

> 5. They know not, neither will they understand; they walk on in darkness all the foundations of the earth are out of course.

> 6. I have said, you are gods; and all of you are children of the most High.

> 7. But you shall die like men, and fall like one of the princes.

Here is what Asaph (the writer of this psalm) is saying; you were created by God and filled with God's power, His glory, and His spirit. So thus, the essence of God rests on you and in you; that is why Jesus says that whatever you pray, if you believe, it will come to pass.

But, Asaph says that we shall die as mere men, and not as children of God that realized who they are, and whose they are-kings and queens dying as mere beggars.

Have an active prayer life (deep conversations with God), and watch your life turn around; from living a life of defeat to being an overcomer and experiencing good success.

PRAY.........PRAY.........PRAY!!! Pray until something happens!!

Read this scripture, claim it, and pray it every day, and watch your life change and be turned around!

This is a promise of God! Deuteronomy 28: 1-13:

> 1. And it shall come to pass, if you shall hearken diligently unto the voice of the Lord your God, to observe and to do all his commandments which I command you this day, that the Lord your God will set you on high above all nations of the earth:

> 2. And all these blessings shall come on you, and overtake you, if you shall hearken unto the voice of the Lord your God.

> 3. Blessed shall you be in the city, and blessed shall you be in the field.

> 4. Blessed shall by the fruit of your body, and the fruit of your ground, and the fruit of your cattle, the increase of your kine, and the flocks of your sheep.

> 5. Blessed shall be your basket and your store.

> 6. Blessed shall you be when you come in, and blessed shall you be when you go out.

7. The Lord shall cause your enemies that rise up against you to be smitten before your face they shall come out against you one way, and flee before you seven ways.

8. The Lord shall command the blessing upon you in your storehouses, and in all that you set your hand unto; and he shall bless you in the land which the Lord your God gave you.

9. The Lord shall establish you an holy people unto himself, as he has sworn unto you, if you shall keep the commandment of the Lord your /God, and walk in his ways.

10. And all people of the earth shall see that you are called by the name of the Lord; and they shall be afraid of you.

11. And the Lord shall make you plenteous in goods, in the fruit of your body, and in the fruit of your cattle, and in the fruit of your ground, a=in the land which the Lord swore unto your fathers to give you.

12. The Lord shall open unto you his good treasure, the heaven to give you the rain unto your land in his season, and to bless all the work of your hand: and you shall lend unto many nations, and you shall not borrow.

13. And the Lord shall make you the head, and not the tail; and you shall be above only, and you shall not be beneath; if that you hearken unto the commandments of the Lord your God, which I command you this day, to observe and to do them:

And even-though my ordeal is not completely over, I still expect to come out victorious because God honors His word.

Remember, you are supposed to do well; so pray, have a daily intimate conversation with your heavenly Father, and read the above scripture every day to remind you of what your position is supposed to be.

What we are doing is giving God's word back to Him! God you said that I am blessed and that I am the head and not the tail; you said that I am a lender and not a borrower.

Why should you operate in His word? Because He honors what He has said. Note Isaiah 55: 10-12:

> 10. For as the rain comes down, and the snow from heaven, and returns not here, but waters the earth, and makes it give seed to the sower, and bread to the eater:

> 11. So shall my word be that goes forth out of my mouth: it shall not return unto me void, but it shall accomplish that which I please, and it shall prosper in the thing whereto I sent it.

> 12. For you shall go out with joy, and be led forth with peace: the mountains and the hills shall break forth before you into singing, and all the trees of the field shall clap their hands.

Let your prayers line up with what He has said in His Word, and then wait on it; then what you have asked, will soon come to pass because He honors His word-It will not be void.

Look what Jesus says in Matthew 24: 35:

> Heaven and earth shall pass away, but my words shall not pass away.

> Pray His words back to Him, and it shall accomplish what you ask in prayer!!

A powerful example of the necessity and power of prayer is recorded in the book of Acts 16: 25-26:

> 25. And at midnight Paul and Silas prayed, and sang praises unto God: and the prisoners heard them.

> 26. And suddenly there was a great earthquake, so that the foundations of the prison were shaken and immediately all the doors were opened, and every one's bands were loosed.

Prayer released them from prison, so imagine what it can do with your situation. The possibilities are endless.

A prayer meeting between two people in jail moved God in heaven-Things happen when you pray!

ALWAYS HAVE A PRAYER LIFE-IT WORKS!

DURING PRAYER, YOU TAKE God's WORD AND GIVE IT BACK TO HIM, FOR HE SAYS THAT HIS WORD WILL NOT RETURN TO HIM VOID-Isaiah 55: 11

Chapter Seven

LEARN HOW TO WAITE ON GOD

I've been out of the hospital a little over a month now; my foot and leg swelling has gone down, but there still remain a deep one inch hole now the size of a small marble, in my toe, but it is getting better with each passing day-at least that is what I tell myself, and the nurses that make home visits also confirm. Yes, I still have those doctors saying that I am simply putting off the inevitable, but I've heard that before:

I had injured my neck and had a herniated disc. When I sneezed, it would knock the disc out and my neck would instantly become painful and stiff. I'd have to turn my entire body to look from side to side. The doctors put me in the hospital and told me that I needed surgery. When they explained to me all that the surgical procedure entailed, I checked myself out of the hospital. The doctor told me that I was simply putting off the inevitable-that was over thirty years ago. God healed me then and I believe that He will do it again with this marble size infected sore on my toe.

God did it once and I believe that He will do it again. So, I stand waiting on His healing and deliverance.

I now have a new testimony, and you cannot have a testimony without first having been tested.

So, learn to wait on Him for He is a very INTENTIONAL God-He has a purpose to what you are going through.

ONE OF THE MOST DIFFICULT THINGS to do in your prayer life is to wait on God to answer your prayers. The reason why it is hard to wait is because we often times wait until our situation is dire before we call on God.

But, waiting is an essential part of your prayer life. Observe Isaiah 40: 29-31:

> 29. He gives power to the faint; and to them that have no might, he increases strength.

> 30. Even the youths shall faint and be weary, and the young men shall utterly fall:

> 31. But they that wait upon the Lord shall renew their strength; they shall mount up with wings as eagles; they shall run, and not be weary; and they shall walk, and not faint.

Isaiah starts out by illustrating the mighty power of God. He empowers the faint hearted (those that feel like quitting), and those that have lost their strength, He strengthens them.

His point is that sometimes you will get weak and tired, but he says to keep on waiting on God to answer your prayer. Isaiah says that the benefits of waiting on God are four fold:

1. Renewed strength- a fresh anointing
2. The ability to fly high like an eagle-rise above your situation
3. The ability to remain steadfast without getting tired
4. The strength to not give up

WAITING IS A PART OF PRAYING!! They go hand in hand

The Apostle Paul discusses the importance of prayer with the Believers in the church at Thessalonica. 1 Thessalonians 5: 16-19:

> 16. Rejoice evermore.
>
> 17. Pray without ceasing.
>
> 18. In everything give thanks: for this is the will of God in Christ Jesus concerning you.
>
> 19. Quench not the spirit.

How do we cease not to pray? Paul says for us to pray continuously. What is he saying?

We keep ourselves in a posture of prayer; whether we are standing, kneeling, walking, running, or just lying down. A posture of prayer is keeping yourself in tuned with the spirit of God, where He pours into you by His spirit; He speaks to you by His spirit. And, in turn, you audibly or mentally talk to Him. Remember, prayer is communing with God-listening and talking; that's why the Apostle Paul says to quench not the spirit of God-don't interfere and stop God from speaking to you.

Why is waiting important during prayer? Our prayer must line up with His will. Sometimes the stuff and the things that we pray for is not in accordance to His will. Sometimes, we ask God for things that are not good for us, that is against His plan and purpose for us.

Learning to patiently wait after praying insures that you "stay connected" to God. In John 15: 5-7, Jesus discussed the importance of staying connect. When you pray and wait, God does what is best for you. Note Jesus conversation to us. John 15: 5-7:

> 5. I am the vine, you are the branches: he that abides in me and I in him, the same brings forth much fruit; for without me you can do nothing.

> 6. If a man abides not in me, he is cast forth as a branch, and is withered; and men gather them, and cast them into the fire, and they are burned.

> 7. If you abide in me, and my words abide in you, you shall ask what you will, and it shall be done unto you.

That is powerful! God will give you whatsoever you desire if you abide (live) in Him.

When you wait on Him, you allow God's will to work in your life and to do what is in your best interest.

We often pray for things and stuff, and situations and conditions that is simply not good for us. Sometimes, we pray for prosperity and wealth, but, oftentimes, that is not good for us. If God gave you everything that you asked for, the things and stuff will separate you from Him.

Sometimes, He answered your prayer, but you reject it because that is not what you asked Him for, but He knew what was best for you. In prayer, sometimes God says yes, no, and not right now-wait. You are many times, not ready for what you are asking Him for; so when you wait on Him, you allow Him to shower His will upon you.

Note what King David said about waiting on God. Psalms 27: 13-14:

13. I had fainted, unless I had believed to see the goodness of the Lord in the land of the living.

14. Wait on the Lord: be of good courage, and he shall strengthen your heart: wait, I say, on the Lord.

Hence, King David is saying to us that if we want to experience the blessing of God among the living, we must endeavor to wait on Him; wait on God's time, for His time works best for you.

Like children, we don't always know what is best for us. Yes, we want to come out of our troublesome situation, or condition, whether it is financial, children, jobs, joy or just peace of mind-we want it, but sometimes God forces us to wait while He does what is best for us.

In the book of Job, it tells us the importance of waiting on God. Job 14: 14

14. If a man dies, shall he live again? All the days of my appointed time will I wait, till my change come.

Job is saying that even though it is uncomfortable, and that he has been in that dire condition for a long time, he has purposed to wait on God to make a change in his life.

Child of God, you have got to learn how to patiently wait on God to bring the changes in your life that you have been praying for.

Yes, we would like for God to move, and move quickly with our prayers, but learning how to wait grooms you in faith.

I know that sometimes it can be hard and difficult, and you want God to come right away, but God knows that that is not always beneficial to us. We acquire strength in waiting, and we learn to trust God when we can't trace Him.

Sometimes God allows us to stay in our valleys a little while; so that when we do get to the mountain, we will appreciate it.

Pray and wait patiently while you maintain your mountain moving faith!

Chapter Eight

YOU MUST FORGIVE-NO MATTER HOW DEEP THE PAIN

When I went into the hospital, I carried a load of hurt and pain in my bosom; pain from what anybody and everybody had wrongfully done to me- and there is no pain like the wounds a pastor carries. I carried it in my bosom like a badge of honor; and though I wouldn't admit it, even to myself, it weighed me down like an iron anchor.

I soon discovered that if I wanted to commune with God and conquer this serious illness, I had to forgive every single person that had hurt me-and there is no hurt like church hurt.

I did, I forgave all that had hurt me, then, and only then did God give me a great degree of peace even in the midst of my storm.

When you don't forgive, you give those that you refuse to forgive power over you. Un-forgiveness holds you in bondage; chained by emotional shackles.

Forgive them, even when you cannot forget the breach. You must choose to forgive, and if you choose to forgive, God will give you the strength to forgive.

I left the hospital with a clean heart, having no anger or malice against any. I had been set free.

Forgiveness is the most powerful act that you will ever do. It is the quintessential of a successful life. Forgiveness is so full of power because you forgive even during the offense while the hurt is still freshly upon you by the perpetrator; and you know definitely that they will hurt you again if given the chance.

Google defines forgive as: to choose to stop feeling angry or resentful towards someone for an offense, flaw, or mistake-like cancelling a debt.

Some say to forgive and forget, but we must forgive even when we cannot forget. You see, God didn't design us to forget. We can't forget the pain that someone caused us-even if we wanted to. God didn't create us to forget; forgetting is a mental flaw; that is why doctors try to treat patients that have memory problems. We were designed to retain the things that we experience in life. It is how we survive-to remember some things that have happened to us, that is, perhaps, detrimental to our health, safety, and wellbeing.

To have a mountain moving faith, you have got to walk in forgiveness; you cannot live a life filled with anger and resentment against someone that has offended you. Yes, it hurts, and your heart is broken while tears scream down you cheeks, but you have got to choose to forgive because, if you don't, it becomes a mountain in your way.

J ESUS HAD A DISCUSSION WITH His disciples on the importance of forgiveness in their lives. He had just taught them to pray, and then, closing out the discussion Jesus goes back to the phrase in the prayer on "forgive us as we forgive others".

Observe what He says: Matthew 6: 14-15-

> 14. For if you forgive men their trespasses, your heavenly Father will also forgive you;

> 15. But if you forgive not men their trespasses, neither will your Father forgive your trespasses.

By this discourse, Jesus displays the importance of forgiveness in our lives. After telling them how to pray, the only part of the prayer that Jesus goes back to is "forgiveness". Hence, He says that to the degree that you forgive others, is the degree that The Heavenly Father forgives you.

When you refuse to forgive, it dilutes your faith! You will never acquire mountain moving faith if you don't forgive those that have hurt you in any way. You must get pass your hurt, resentment, and anger if you want to move some mountains out of your way-oftentimes, un-forgiveness becomes a mountain to you.

You see, the reason why forgiveness is so powerful, is that you forgive even while the pain of what they did to you still resonates in your heart-the scars and the hurt is still there.

You have to choose to forgive in order to move on in your designed purpose by God. You will have a most difficult spiritual and physical journey if you carry that anger, hurt, and resentment in your bosom.

Observe Jesus demonstration of how important forgiveness is. Even while hanging on the cross; his body riddled in pain and drench in blood, He demonstrated the importance of forgiveness; some of His last words- Luke 23: 33-34:

> 33. And when they were come to the place, which is called Calvary, there they crucified him, and the malefactors, one on the right hand, and the other on the left.

> 34. Then said Jesus, Father, forgive them; for they know not what they do

In the midst of all of His suffering and agony, He asked God to forgive them for what they had done to Him.

The reason why forgiveness is so powerful is because you have to choose to forgive even while you are yet bleeding inside from the wounds they afflicted upon; forgive while you are still hurting. Tears rolling down your face, still, forgive. Forgiveness does more for you than for the one that you forgive.

God will pay them for what they have done to you. Note Deuteronomy 32: 35.

To me belongs vengeance, and recompense; their foot shall slide in due time: for the day of their calamity is at hand, and the things that shall come upon them make haste.

In other words, whatever has happened to you, or whatever someone has done to you, just let it go. God is promising that He will repay them for what they have done to you. You just forgive them so that you can continue to go forward and move the mountains in your life.

Galatians 6: 7-9…

> 7. Be not deceived; God is not mocked; for whatsoever a man sows, that shall he also reap.

> 8. For he that sows to his flesh shall of the flesh reap corruption; but he that sows to the Spirit shall of the Spirit reap life everlasting.

> 9. And let us not be weary in well doing: for in due season we shall reap, if we faint not.

The Apostle Paul is saying that you don't have to be angry or resentful for what someone did to you, or the hurt they might have caused because God is going to repay them for what they have done, but you mustn't let it become a mountain to you.

So, choose to forgive the breach that someone has caused. Sometimes, we spent all of our time crying about the doors that have closed on us until we fail to recognize the doors that God opened for you-for He never closes a door without also opening another for you.

So, forgive so that you can have mountain moving faith!!

Chapter Nine

REALIZING GRACE AND MERCY

Sometimes, during the course of our living, we will have to go through some things that we just weren't prepared for. It becomes a mountain, sometimes a lifelong mountain of generational proportions.

Often times, God doesn't move our troubles, but shows us how to get through them; that is where His grace and mercy comes in.

Grace is God giving you what you don't deserve, and mercy is God sparing you from what you deserve.

In my ordeal, I had to learn how to depend on His grace and mercy. In my past, I had lived a riotous life, so I knew that whatever hurt and pain I got through this diabetic sickness, I deserved it. For I had paved the way for the devil to attack me; but God'S grace, and His mercy pleaded my case so I didn't get what I deserved, and was given what I did not deserve.

So, now I live in thankfulness, for my situation could have easily gone the other way, but God's goodness flung grace and mercy my way......and so I stand with a testimony of how He kept me; and remember, you can't have a testimony without first being tested!

THE APOSTLE PAUL GIVES US A snapshot of grace and mercy at work in his second letter to the church of Corinth: 2 Corinthians 12: 7-10-

> 7. And lest I should be exalted above measure through the abundance of the revelations, there was given to me a thorn in the flesh, the messenger of Satan to buffet me, lest I should be exalted above measure.

> 8. For this thing, I sought the Lord three times, that it might depart from me.

> 9. And he said unto me, My grace is sufficient for you, for my strength is made perfect in weakness. Most gladly therefore will I rther glory in my infirmities, that the power fo Christ may rest upn me.

> 10. Therefore I take pleasure in infirmities, in reproaches, in necessities, in persecutions, in distresses for Christ sake ; for when I am weak, then am I strong.

Paul surmises to us that God does not always remove all of the things that are plaguing us; no, sometimes, he allows them to remain, so that we will have to deal with them and rely on His power to help us overcome and conquer that which is a mountain to us.

God tells him that His grace is sufficient, and that His strength is made perfect in weakness. In other words, God is saying, "Keep your eyes and your faith on me. I am all that you will ever need."

His strength is made perfect in weakness means that His strength is developed and completed during your weakest times when that mountain just won't move. God grooms you during those challenging times.

Note, Paul says that Satan sent him a messenger to beat him.

Special note: The devil only sends messages to people that's a threat to him.

If the devil never bothers you, and he never brings something your way that you simply were not ready for, then you probably need to check how you live.

You have got to keep the thought in your bosom that God is a keeper, and He will not allow you to go through it if you can't get through it.

Expect grace and mercy to intercede for you and plead your case for whatever mountain that you are facing in your life.

Closing

Our lives are a continuous journey that is filled with many mountains and deep valleys; a lot of highs and lows. Many of them, The Lord of spirits, designed to assist us in developing who we were supposed to become-to walk in God's purpose and plan for our lives; just as a baby falls many times before it learns to walk.

You don't always have to move the mountain that you are confronted with; sometimes, you can change it; Change that mountain of despair into a mountain of hope filled with dreams. Instead of a mountain of sadness, change it into a mountain of joy.

Whichever, move your mountain, or change your mountain, you have the power resting in you to get rid of that plaguing mountain.

God already knew that your life would be filled with many challenges, so He designed you to be able to overcome them with something that you already have, but oftentimes ignore it.

Note what Jesus says in John 7: 37-38:

> 37. In the last day, that great day of the feast, Jesus stood and cried, saying, if any man thirst, let him come unto me, and drink.

> 38. He that believes on me, as the scripture has said, out of his belly shall flow rivers of living water.

Jesus is saying to you that deep inside of you is a well of power that you can tap into that can change your life and others around you. You've got a deep well of power inside of you and somebody ought to be drinking from your well-your power is not just for you, but it is also to assist others.

We cannot entirely blame this young generation, generation X, that's coming on behind the Baby Boomers because they have been drinking from the Baby Boomers well-thus, they become as the Boomers were. Our children often are simply a replica of us; what they are, we taught them-good or bad.

Speak to your situation, and tell it, by faith, to be removed, then "expect" it to move. Jesus said that you will have whatever you believe. It's already there waiting for you to speak mountain moving faith into existence.

If you continue to walk and believe like you always have, then you will get the results that you have always gotten.

Mountain moving faith is not about you or who you are, or where you are from; it's bigger than you. It is the power of God resting inside of you.

Speak it

Believe it

Expect it

And it shall come to pass!!

Now say this aloud and put it into the atmosphere-Directed at whatever is plaguing you-whatever need, desire, sickness, just whatever it is that you are going through right now.

"MOUTAIN, BE REMOVED AND GET OUT OF MY WAY. I CONQUER YOU BY THE POWER OF GOD THROUGH FAITH!!!"

Well, it has been about two months since I have been out of the hospital listening to all the grave news from the doctors, and all of the "want to be" neighborhood doctors. Everything that they said wouldn't and couldn't happen did happen.

When I went back to the surgeon's office, he looked at my foot in utter amazement and said in disbelief:

"This is not the same foot that I saw in the hospital!" He said in disbelief, as he rubbed his hand across his face.

"Yea, it is," I said, beaming like a little kid on Christmas day that got everything that he wanted.

He yelled down the hall at his assistant, the other doctor that wanted to amputate my foot.

He entered the room and didn't say anything, but you could see amazement written all over is face.

This moment was worth all that I had gone through. It loudly proclaimed to them that God is real-real enough to come by the hospital room of one of His preachers and heal a leg that was plagued because of an infected wound the size of a quarter. Now, every time I pick up a quarter, I smile and whisper to myself, "Won't He do it."

Printed in the United States
by Baker & Taylor Publisher Services